BADGES OF THE BRITISH ARMY
1820 TO THE PRESENT
An illustrated reference guide
for collectors

BADGES OF
THE BRITISH ARMY
1820 TO THE PRESENT
An illustrated reference guide
for collectors

F. Wilkinson

ARMS AND ARMOUR PRESS

Published in Great Britain
in 1987 by Arms & Armour Press Limited,
Artillery House, Artillery Row, London SW1P 1RT.

Distributed in the USA by Sterling Publishing Co. Inc.,
2 Park Avenue, New York, NY 10016.

Distributed in Australia by
Capricorn Link (Australia) Pty. Ltd., P.O. Box 665,
Lane Cove, New South Wales 2066, Australia.

Reprinted 1989

British Library Cataloguing in Publication Data
Wilkinson, Frederick
Badges of the British Army 1820 to the present: an
illustrated reference guide for collectors. – 7th ed. –
(Illustrated reference guides for collectors)
1. Great Britain. *Army* – Medals, badges, decoration.
etc. – Pictorial works.   I. Title   II. Series
355.1'4   UC535.G7

ISBN 0-85368-789-7

Photography by Paul Forrester

Designed by David Gibbons; edited by Michael Boxall;
typeset by Typesetters (Birmingham) Ltd.; printed and bound
in Great Britain by Biddles Ltd, Guildford and King's Lynn

CONTENTS

Preface   7

Introduction   9

Bibliography   15

Price Guide   17

THE PLATES: 21
Shoulder belt plates   22–5
Headdress plates   26–7
Collar dogs and waist belt clasps   28–9
Buttons and sundry items   30–1
Badges of 'The Queen's'   32–3
Fusiliers' grenades   34–5
RAF and Airborne Forces   36–7
Crosses and London units   38–9
Scottish units   40–1, 60–1
Artillery units   42–3
Marines and Militia   44–5
The Middlesex Regiment   44–5
Corps and Proficiency badges   46–7
London units   48–9
Guards units   50–1
Armoured and Cavalry units   52–3
Cavalry units   54–5
Irish units   58–9
County Regiments and Women's units   62–5
County Regiments, Yeomanry and miscellaneous
    units   66–75
Corps and miscellaneous badges   76–7

Index to the Plates   78

PREFACE

This book first appeared in 1969 and has since run to six editions. The author and publishers feel that it is now time to produce a new version incorporating knowledge and experience gained during the intervening period.

The book differs from previous editions in that it attempts to extend its coverage by including a few badges that, perhaps, do not fall strictly within the original scope. This has been done to indicate some less obvious fields of badge collecting, for it is a sad fact that the popularity of badges has led to an increase in prices and this restricts the opportunities of many collectors. Another very unfortunate result of this great interest has been the increased production of fakes, copies and restrikes. In the early days these copies were reasonably easy to spot, but sadly the skill of the producers has increased to such a degree that it is often difficult to be sure that any item is genuine and original. All the badges illustrated are originals, the majority having been collected long before restrikes appeared in quantity.

The layout of the book has also been changed, the items being arranged differently in the hope that it will prove easier for the reader to identify and value badges. In a book of this size it is impossible to do more than show a selection of the tremendous variety of badges, and a bibliography has been included for those who wish to extend their interest.

The dates included in the captions show the period for which the badges were generally in use, but it must be stressed that in many cases regiments did not always comply with new regulations and continued to wear badges that were officially out of date.

Once again the author is indebted to Jim Burgess who cheerfully disorganized his home, and his collection in order that it could be photographed. His trust and kindness are greatly appreciated.

The photographs were taken by Paul Forrester who has long suffered the author's photographic demands. On this occasion faulty film and other problems added to his heavy burden. As always, he overcame all difficulties with good humour and professional competence.

Finally the author must thank Laurie Archer who, over the years, has proved a staunch friend, answering queries and providing authoritative information on a range of obscure badges and other topics with superb expertise and good humour.

F. Wilkinson, London, 1987

INTRODUCTION

The standardization of badges in the British Army dates from the eighteenth century. Prior to this, regiments were usually known by the name of their colonel or commanding officer. Badges varied, but often incorporated the coat-of-arms of the colonel. A change of commanding officer meant a change of title and probably a change of badge.

In 1751 an order was issued which saw the introduction of a more standard system of identifying units. Infantry regiments were numbered and some were allowed to incorporate authorized special designs as part of their badges. By this date, symbols such as the dragon, the white horse of Hanover and the Prince of Wales's Feathers were already in use and were to remain with various regiments right up to the present. Mottoes were also incorporated in badges and at this early date the most common was *Nec Espera Terrent* (Nor do Difficulties Deter).

These badges and mottoes were mostly worn on the various styles of head-dress, usually embroidered on the cloth caps, but they also appeared on another piece of equipment – the shoulder belt plate (see **1–14**). This item of uniform developed during the later part of the 18th century when the belt was moved from the waist to cross the chest and shoulders. At first the plates were usually small, oval and fairly simple, but later ones were rectangular and much more elaborate. Those for the other ranks were normally of stamped brass and most were impressed or engraved with the regimental number. Later, name, crest, motto and often battle honours were included. Those for the officers were much more elaborate and were made up of several components held together by pierced lugs and thin wire.

Various styles of head-dress had been worn by the infantry at different periods, but in 1800 the famous shako, known from its cylindrical shape as the stovepipe, was adopted. At the front was fitted a large rectangular metal badge, and as usual there was a difference in quality between those worn by officers and those worn by other ranks. The basic plate had the crowned royal cypher GR, together with military trophies, but regiments with special emblems were allowed to include them on the plate. In 1812 the style of shako was changed and the plate became smaller and was shaped like a shield, but like its predecessor, displayed the royal cipher and often had some regimental distinctions (see **4**).

This style of head-dress underwent various modifications as changing fashion led to its becoming bell-topped, and then cylindrical again with the advent of the Albert shako in 1844. The style of badge was also changed, becoming star-shaped and much more elaborate.

In 1855 the shoulder belt plate was abolished except for Scottish units, and in the same year a low crowned shako was adopted. This, in a variety of forms, lasted until 1878 when the Home Service Pattern Helmet was introduced. This cloth and cork helmet had a large, elaborate, star-shaped badge and a top central spike or, for the corps, a ball-and-cup fitting. Like previous styles of badge, those for other ranks were usually of stamped brass while those for officers were made up of several components (see **16**).

In 1874 a new style of undress cap, the glengarry, was adopted and this had its own badge which usually had the regimental number within a circlet. Until 1881 almost all army badges had carried the regimental number, but in that year far-sweeping reforms of the army were introduced by Lord Cardwell. Numbers were discarded and names substituted, and in 1885 the glengarry was abandoned.

Cavalry head-dress has nearly always been much more elaborate than that of the infantry and in consequence the badges were usually larger and more decorative. The lancers, introduced in the early 19th century, wore a distinctive *tschapka* cap which was based on the head-dress of the Polish lancers and had a large crescent-shaped plate. The Lifeguards and other mounted units wore metal helmets, often surmounted by plumes and with large central front plates. Today's armoured and mobile units, which are the descendants of the cavalry, regiments, wear badges that are little different from those of the infantry.

Distinction must be made between the various sections of the armed forces. In addition to the standing regular army there were the militia, the volunteers, the yeomanry and later the Territorial Army. Each group wore badges similar to those of the regulars, but often differing in details; consequently, identification can be difficult. One guiding feature is that the basic colour of badges for regular army units was 'gold', while for milita it was 'silver'. This rule of thumb must be used cautiously: most Scottish units also favour 'silver' badges.

The vast majority of badges offered to the collector will date from the mid to late nineteenth century onwards, and dating them can be a problem, but there are some general rules which can often help. It should be stressed, however, that these rules are only guides and there are exceptions to all of them. The crown is the first indication of date. Badges of Queen Victoria's reign (1837–1901) will have a queen's crown with its dome-shaped appearance (see **19**). Badges of King Edward VIII (1901–10), George V (1910–36) and George VI (1936–52) had the crown changed (see **16**) and this type is known as the king's crown. The accession of Queen Elizabeth II in 1952 saw the adoption of another style of crown and to distinguish between the two queens that of Victoria is usually abbreviated to QVC.

If the badge incorporates a regimental number it probably pre-dates 1881 when the reforms abandoning numbers were introduced. Regimental titles have changed over the years and these, too, can help date a piece. Obviously the style of badge is a vital dating feature, and reference to the examples illustrated may give some guidance in the identifying of similar pieces. Mottoes can also be helpful although some are used by more than one regiment.

The most commonly used materials in badge manufacture were gilding metal, usually described as brass by many collectors (as it is in this book), and white metal. Those badges composed of both are described as bimetal), while many officers' badges were of bronze. In times of shortage, as happened during the World Wars, some badges were produced in an economy style; those which had usually been of bimetal were made in brass. During the Second World War brass was often replaced by plastic. In 1952 a new material, usually referred to as Staybrite, was introduced. This anodized aluminium gave the badges a rather gaudy, cheap appearance and they are generally unpopular, but they are a cheap starting-point for a collector of limited means!

While metal badges are the most sought after, there are many interesting cloth badges, although they are often in poor condition, the material being more susceptible to damage. Again, one or two examples have been included.

Restrikes struck from original dies or copied from originals using modern hi-tech methods have become a major hazard for the badge collector and today their quality is extremely high. Detection can be very difficult and is largely a matter of experience. This statement is easy to make, but for the collector experience is a difficult thing to acquire. One of the best ways is to haunt the dealers, markets, auction houses, collecting societies and museums, taking every opportunity to look at and, above all, to handle badges. Look at the degree and position of wear, look at the back and observe how the lugs or sliders are fitted and observe the quality of the detail. Whenever possible compare the restrike with known originals or with photographs of the genuine piece and it may be possible to pinpoint minor differences. If the collector is happy to have a copy of a rare badge, there can be no objection to restrikes, but if the aim is to acquire original badges, restrikes are not appropriate. There is also the problem of the unscrupulous or unknowing dealer who tries to sell a restrike as an original. In the end the old adage *Caveat emptor* (Let the buyer beware) is probably the best advice. If a collector finds a good reliable dealer ready to offer guarantees, he has found a 'treasure'.

The majority of badges illustrated are from British Army head-dress, but there were other types including proficiency badges, collar badges (commonly known as dogs), shoulder titles and divisional signs. All have their collectors and a few examples have been included. Fortunately there are now a number of authoritative books dealing with these themes and the collector will find them listed in the bibliography.

Badge collecting lends itself to many approaches and the collector may well find that his original concept becomes modified as knowledge and the collection grow. It is probably true to say that most collectors begin with the object of putting together a large collection of badges with little idea of making any selection. This somewhat 'jackdaw' approach often changes as a particular interest begins to develop, and some collectors begin to specialize. The number of options is very large. Some concentrate on one particular regiment and seek to acquire as many of its badges as possible. The group on Plate **6** is an example of the variety of badges used by one unit, yet that particular collection is far from complete. Another approach is to concentrate on a particular campaign and seek out badges of those regiments that served in it. Theme collections can be made with the aim of acquiring badges with a common feature such as animals, coats-of-arms, plants or castles. Yet another approach might be to specialize in a period and collect units that were serving in the 1950s, for example.

Once a theme or period has been selected the obvious question is, where does the collector look for the material? The days when most markets or antique shops had a 'junk' box, which often held a few badges at prices well within a youthful enthusiast's pocket, have long since gone. The very popularity of badge collecting has forced prices up and the hobby is now quite big business and this in turn has attracted some dealers who are, perhaps, not quite as careful as they might be, and who do not always describe their wares as accurately as they should.

One of the greatest hazards for the modern collector is the restrike. As suggested, if a collector is satisfied to have a modern copy in his collection there is no problem. The infuriating thing is to find that the 'rare' badge, which cost a fair amount and seemed so genuine, is only a restrike. It would be less than honest to suggest that it is easy to spot these impostors; many a well-established collector has been misled. It must be said yet again that the only defences are experience and a reliable supplier.

Some dealers offer a guarantee and they should be supported. There is also an implied guarantee by the auction houses most of whom will refund the purchase price if a badge can be shown to be not as catalogued. Apart from the auction houses and specialist dealers, the other sources are the obvious ones of fellow collectors, antique-shops and markets. There are several societies devoted to badge collecting and associated topics, and a subscription to these is well worthwhile for the contacts, advice and information contained in their newsletters or magazines. Jumble sales, boot sales and the street markets are also worth some attention although it must be said that these are no longer the happy hunting-grounds they once were.

Perseverance is an essential characteristic of the badge collector, but the pleasure of finding a desirable badge will be reward enough and may help to compensate for all the fruitless searches.

Displaying the collection is very much a personal choice, but whichever method is used the prime consideration must be the preservation of the badge. The old methods of nailing them to boards, drilling holes in the slider, bending and twisting lugs and even breaking them off must be avoided at all costs. One simple method is to mount them on card or polystyrene tiles which can be covered with material or painted, and cut to accommodate the sliders and lugs. Mounted in glazed frames, they make attractive wall decorations. Shallow drawers are convenient, but the badges are obviously less easily viewed. Before any display is mounted it is most important to plan the lay-out, remembering to leave gaps for any badges that may be needed to complete a sequence.

Most collectors like to clean their badges and there are many proprietary polishes on the market, the least abrasive should always be used to reduce wear on the badge. Some collectors like to lacquer their cleaned badges, but many deplore the idea. It should be pointed out that many lacquers discolour and crack and some can be very difficult to remove. On balance it is probably better not to lacquer, but obviously each collector must reach his own conclusion.

However the badges are displayed, it is important to compile a comprehensive catalogue, preferably with photographs. Not only is it useful for reference, but it will also be invaluable for insurance; it can be a shock to discover how the value of a collection has grown. It is worth considering the use of one of the invisible security inks to mark the badges so that positive identification is assured in the event of recovery from loss or theft.

Badge collecting is still one of the cheaper hobbies and can stimulate all manner of interests and encourage research into so many fields such as weapons, uniforms, medals, regimental histories, biographies, campaigns, war games and social history. Above all it is a hobby that will offer its supporters many hours of pleasure, the chance to meet fellow enthusiasts and even, on rare occasions, some financial benefit.

BIBLIOGRAPHY

Anon. *Badges and Emblems of the British Forces 1940.* London, 1968

Almack, E. *Regimental Badges worn in the British Army 100 years ago.* London, 1970

Bloomer, W., and Bloomer, K. *Badges of the Highland and Lowland Regiments.* London, 1982

— *Scottish Regimental Badges 1793–1971.* London, 1982

Carman, W. Y. *Glengarry Badges of the British Line Regiments to 1881.* London, 1973

Chichester, H., and Burgess-Short, G. *Records and Badges of Every Regiment and Corps in the British Army.* (repr.) London, 1986

Churchill, C., and Westlake, R. *British Army Collar Badges 1881 to the Present.* London, 1986

Cole, H. N. *Badges on Battledress.* London, 1953

Cox, R. H. W. *Military Badges of the British Empire.* London, 1982

Edwards, T. J. *Regimental Badges.* London, 1968

Gaylor, J. *Military Badge Collecting.* London, 1977

Kipling, A. L., and King, H. L. *Head-Dress Badges of the British Army.* vol 1, London, 1978; vol 2, London, 1979

May, W., Carman, W. and Tanner, J. *Badges and Insignia of the British Armed Services.* London, 1974

Mollo, A., and McGregor, M. *Naval, Marine and Air Force Uniforms of World War 2.* London, 1975

Norman, C. B. *Battle Honours of the British Army.* London, 1911

Parkyn, H. G. *Shoulder Belt Plates and Buttons.* Aldershot, 1956

Rawlings, K. *British Military Badges.* Bournemouth, 1977

Ripley, H. *Buttons of the British Army 1855–1970.* London, 1971

Rosignoli, G. *Army Badges and Insignia of World War 2.* vol 1, London, 1972; vol 2, London, 1975

— *Army Badges and Insignia since 1945.* London, 1973

— *Air Force Badges and Insignia of World War 2.* London, 1976

Westlake, R. *A Register of Territorial Force Cadet Units 1910–22.* Wembley, 1984

— *The Rifle Volunteers.* Chippenham, 1982

— *The Territorial Battalions.* Tunbridge Wells, 1986

White, A. S. *A Bibliography of the Regimental Histories of the British Army.* London, 1965

Periodicals which have occasional articles about badges

Journal of Military Historical Society

Journal of the Society for Army Historical Research

Military Illustrated

Military Modelling

PRICE GUIDE

Like all such lists this must be treated with caution. It was compiled in the light of current market conditions, and represents prices likely to be asked by a professional dealer offering the genuine article in reasonably good condition. By the time it is in print it may already be a little out of date; fluctuations in demand can cause unexpected changes in value. For the dedicated collector it should be used in conjuction with price lists from the auctioneers since many dealers obtain their stock from auctions. The price they pay will obviously not be the price that they ask for they have a quite legitimate profit margin or 'mark up' which can be as high as 100%. It should be borne in mind that nothing has a fixed definitive value; any item is worth only what somebody is prepared to pay for it!

1.	£200	21.	£5	41.	£2
2.	£200	22.	£5	42.	£2
3.	£250	23.	£4	43.	£30
4.	£200	24.	£30	44.	£3
5.	£250	25.	£3	45.	£2
6.	£280	26.	£1	46.	£2
7.	£220	27.	£2	47.	£3
8.	£300	28.	£5	48.	£1
9.	£200	29.	£5	49.	£1
10.	£280	30.	£3	50.	£1
11.	£250	31.	£50	51.	£3
12.	£320	32.	£3	52.	£40
13.	£220	33.	£2	53.	£1
14.	£200	34.	£20	54.	£1
15.	£100	35.	£50	55.	£1
16.	£120	36.	£50	56.	£8
17.	£80	37.	£50	57.	£95
18.	£60	38.	£1	58.	£85
19.	£50	39.	£3	59.	£2
20.	£50	40.	£3	60.	£3

61. £7	108. £9	156. £7
62. £4	109. £12	157. £1
63. £4	110. £38	158. £2
64. £18	111. £12	159. £22
65. £12	112. £12	160. £15
66. £5	113. £12	161. £12
67. £50	114. £5	162. £2
68. £4	115. £10	163. £3
69. £3	116. £12	164. £12
70. £5	117. £7	165. £7
71. £6	118. £15	166. £12
72. £60	119. £10	167. £12
73. £45	120. £6	168. £6
74. £50	121. £5	169. £8
75. £50	122. £12	170. £10
76. £50	123. £10	171. £6
77. £65	124. £15	172. £45
78. £65	125. £15	173. £10
79. £65	126. £15	174. £15
80. £65	127. £6	175. £12
81. £12	128. £55	176. £20
82. £10	129. £48	177. £6
83. £5	130. £10	178. £10
84. £3	131. £17	179. £9
85. £3	132. £7	180. £9
86. £5	133. £2	181. £11
87. £15	134/135. £2	182. £5
88. £5	136. £3	183. £13
89. £9	137. £45	184. £3
90. £5	138. £50	185. £10
91. £70	139. £9	186. £4
92. £8	140. £4	187. £3
93. £3	141. £12	188. £4
94. £10	142. £24	189. £4
95. £5	143. £32	190. £4
96. £15	144. £12	191. £4
97. £4	145. £100	192. £4
98. £17	146. £15	193. £5
99. £15	147. £8	194. £10
100. £10	148. £7	195. £20
101. £10	149. £4	196. £2
102. £7	150. £7	197. £4
103. £5	151. £5	198. £10
104. £7	152. £3	199. £25
105. £12	153. £6	200. £6
106. £12	154. £2	201. £4
107. £14	155. £3	202. £16

203. £50	250. £8	297. £15
204. £6	251. £10	298. £6
205. £35	252. £6	299. £6
206. £8	253. £12	300. £5
207. £25	254. £18	301. £8
208. £11	255. £9	302. £20
209. £5	256. £8	303. £4
210. £3	257. £9	304. £6
211. £6	258. £26	305. £8
212. £20	259. £6	306. £6
213. £13	260. £4	307. £10
214. £10	261. £2	308. £5
215. £10	262. £11	309. £20
216. £3	263. £65	310. £10
217. £1	264. £18	311. £5
218. £15	265. £15	312. £10
219. £15	266. £20	313. £6
220. £6	267. £30	314. £12
221. £9	268. £22	315. £4
222. £3	269. £25	316. £22
223. £16	270. £5	317. £13
224. £12	271. £18	318. £5
225. £10	272. £45	319. £6
226. £8	273. —	320. £5
227. £15	274. £20	321. £5
228. £19	275. £18	322. £8
229. £10	276. £9	323. £5
230. £15	277. £13	324. £15
231. £8	278. £12	325. £10
232. £8	279. £5	326. £10
233. £18	280. £4	327. £20
234. £18	281. £4	328. £12
235. £30	282. £5	329. £9
236. £12	283. £3	330. £10
237. £5	284. £6	331. £35
238. £10	285. £5	332. £7
239. £10	286. £2	333. £10
240. £9	287. £5	334. £12
241. £25	288. £5	335. £5
242. £9	289. £5	336. £6
243. £5	290. £4	337. £10
244. £18	291. £12	338. £19
245. £25	292. £4	339. £15
246. £10	293. £5	340. £10
247. £10	294. £8	341. £16
248. £25	295. £3	342. £12
249. £15	296. £4	343. £24

344.	£4	375.	£10	406.	£5
345.	£4	376.	£12	407.	£5
346.	£10	377.	£10	408.	£5
347.	£10	378.	£10	409.	£7
348.	£3	379.	£5	410.	£5
349.	£5	380.	£6	411.	£8
350.	£5	381.	£4	412.	£5
351.	£10	382.	£8	413.	£7
352.	£10	383.	£5	414.	£9
353.	£20	384.	£8	415.	£7
354.	£4	385.	£12	416.	£8
355.	£4	386.	£10	417.	£4
356.	£15	387.	£5	418.	£5
357.	£8	388.	£11	419.	£7
358.	£6	389.	£10	420.	£5
359.	£4	390.	£3	421.	£1
360.	£3	391.	£30	422.	£3
361.	£10	392.	£5	423.	£10
362.	£15	393.	£4	424.	£25
363.	£10	394.	£5	425.	£6
364.	£8	395.	£45	426.	£10
365.	£6	396.	£30	427.	£5
366.	£7	397.	£5	428.	£5
367.	£5	398.	£5	429.	£8
368.	£8	399.	£5	430.	£6
369.	£10	400.	£7	431.	£12
370.	£5	401.	£5	432.	£35
371.	£6	402.	£7	433.	£5
372.	£5	403.	£3	434.	£5
373.	£5	404.	£5	435.	£5
374.	£5	405.	£8	436.	£8

BADGES OF THE BRITISH ARMY
1820 TO THE PRESENT

1. The 17th (Leicestershire) Regiment of Foot. Other ranks' shoulder belt plate, late 18th century. Brass.
2. The 11th (North Devon) Regiment of Foot. Other ranks' shoulder belt plate, 18th century. Brass.
3. The Devizes Association (early 19th-century volunteer unit). Shoulder belt plate, incorporating castle from town's coat of arms. Gilded brass.
4. Officers' helmet plate for the 1812, Waterloo Pattern shako. Gilded. Regiments with special badges had the emblems impressed below a smaller cipher.
5. London and Westminster Light Horse Volunteers. Shoulder belt plate, late 18th century. White metal.
6. The Royal East India Volunteers, 2nd Regiment (London volunteer unit). Shoulder belt plate. Gilded, hallmarked for 1796.
7. The Loyal Chelmsford Volunteers (formed 1803). Shoulder belt plate. Gilded.
8. The 2nd (Queen's Royal) Regiment of Foot. Officers' shoulder belt plate. Silver, hallmarked for 1791.

9

10

12

13

9. The 62nd (The Wiltshire) Regiment of Foot. Other ranks' shoulder belt plate, *circa* 1840. Stamped brass.
10. The 41st (Welch) Regiment of Foot. Officers' shoulder belt plate. The blue enamel centre was introduced in 1831.
11. The 9th (The East Norfolk) Regiment of Foot. Shoulder belt plate. The separate figure of Britannia is pinned to the plate. Brass.
12. The 25th (The King's Own Borderers) Regiment of Foot. Elaborate shoulder belt plate, *circa* 1850. A slider was also worn on the belt.
13. The 9th (The East Norfolk) Regiment of Foot. Other ranks' shoulder belt plate. Pressed brass.
14. The 86th (Royal County Down) Regiment of Foot. Other ranks' shoulder belt plate, *circa* 1850. It was attached to the belt by four broad hooks instead of the more usual two hooks and two lugs. Pressed brass.

15

16

18

19

15. The Bloomsbury Rifles, raised in 1860; later became a Volunteer Battalion in The Rifle Brigade. Bronze-coloured helmet plate.

16. The Norfolk Regiment. Home Service Pattern helmet plate. Central Britannia and motto in white metal. King's crown dates this to post-1902.

17. The Norfolk Regiment. Other ranks' shako plate with typical double dome of Queen Victoria's crown (QVC); worn 1869–79.

18. The 24th County of London Battalion. Home Service Pattern helmet plate with King's crown; central paschal lamb mounted on red material.

19. The 4th Volunteer Battalion, The Queen's Royal West Surrey Regiment. Belt fitting with QVC and a threaded screw fitting. White metal.

20. The 7th City of London Battalion, The London Regiment. Formed in 1908. Other ranks' Full Dress helmet plate.

21

22

23

25

26

27

28

29

30

32

33

34

36

37

24

31

35

38

21. The Tank Corps. One of a pair of opposite-facing collar badges or 'dogs'.
22. The Northamptonshire Regiment. Collar badge.
23. The Lincolnshire Regiment. Collar badge.
24. The 4th Volunteer Battalion, The Royal West Surrey Regiment. Shooting badge worn on left sleeve of tunic. White metal.
25. The King's Own (Royal Lancaster Regiment). Collar dog.
26. Royal Air Force Volunteer Reserve. Collar dog. Brass.
27. The Gordon Highlanders. Collar dog.
28. The Bloomsbury Rifles. Collar dog, *circa* 1900. White metal.
29. The 7th City of London Battalion. Flaming grenade collar dog.
30. The Norfolk Regiment. Collar dog.
31. The 10th (North Lincoln) Regiment of Foot. Waist belt clasp, pre-1881. Bimetal.
32. Oxford University Officer's Training Corps (Cavalry). Collar dog. White metal.
33. The Hertfordshire and Bedfordshire Yeomanry. Collar dog. Bimetal.
34. The 80th (Staffordshire Volunteers) Regiment of Foot. Numeral worn on the round, 'pork-pie' Undress cap. Brass.
35. The 66th (Berkshire) Regiment of Foot. Waist belt clasp, pre-1881. Bimetal.
36. The Norfolk Regiment. Waist belt clasp, *circa* 1900. Bimetal.
37. The Norfolk Regiment. Waist belt clasp, pre-1881.
38. The Royal Fusiliers. Victorian waist belt clasp.

39   40   41   42

44   45   46   47

48   49   50   51

53   54   55

43

52

56

39. The Duke of Cornwall's Light Infantry. Other ranks' tunic button, post-1929.
40. Royal Engineers' Department. Officers' button with QVC and cipher. Gilded.
41. Although similar to military buttons, this is an early London Post Office button.
42. Ordnance Store. Officers' button, *circa* 1880. Gilded.
43. The Westminster Volunteers. Belt fitting, 19th century. White metal.
44. General Officers' button, 19th century. Gilded.
45. Oxford University Rifle Volunteers (OURV). Button, mid 19th century. White metal.
46. Medical Staff. Officers' button, *circa* 1880. Gilded.
47. Cinque Port Rifle Volunteers. Button, late 19th century. White metal.
48. The Royal Air Force. Other ranks' button, pre-1953. Brass.
49. RAF. Officers' button of same period.
50. The Air Training Corps. Button. White metal.
51. The Holborn Battalion, The Rifle Volunteers. Lapel badge.
52. The 38th Corps of Rifle Volunteers (formed in 1860). Belt fitting. As this badge uses the title 'Artists' it must postdate 1877 when this distinction was introduced.
53. British Airborne Forces. Shoulder patch, Second World War. Cloth.
54. Lapel brooch for those who rendered special services during the First World War; each is numbered on the back. White metal.
55. London Metropolitan Special Constabulary. Cap badge, pre-1953. White metal.
56. The 28th County of London Battalion (Artists Rifles). Second pattern badge.

57

58

61

63

64

67

68

66

69

70

71

57. The 2nd (Queen's Royal) Regiment of Foot. Shako plate. Bimetal.
58. The Second (Queen's Royal) Regiment of Foot. Shako plate, Brass.
59. Regimental numeral. Brass.
60. Shoulder title. Brass.
61. Badge adopted in 1924. Gilding metal.
62. 4th Volunteer Battalion of the regiment. White metal.
63. Forage cap badge, 1898–1921. Bimetal.
64. 22nd County of London Battalion (The Queen's). 1908–22.
65. Cranleigh School Cadet Force. One of the Officer's Training Corps, known from 1948 as the Combined Cadet Force.
66. Badge worn as a unit of the Territorial Force, 1908–21. Blackened brass.
67. The 3rd Volunteer Battalion, The East Surrey Regiment. With QVC. Bronze.
68. The Queen's Regiment. Badge introduced in 1966. Anodized.
69. Collar dog of this regiment, worn 1908–22.
70. Badge of The Queen's Royal Surrey Regiment, formed when The Queen's Royal Regiment (West Surrey) and The East Surrey Regiment were amalgamated in 1959. Anodized.
71. Another version of the collar dog.
72. The 4th Volunteer Battalion, The East Surrey Regiment. Bronze.

73

74

76

78

79

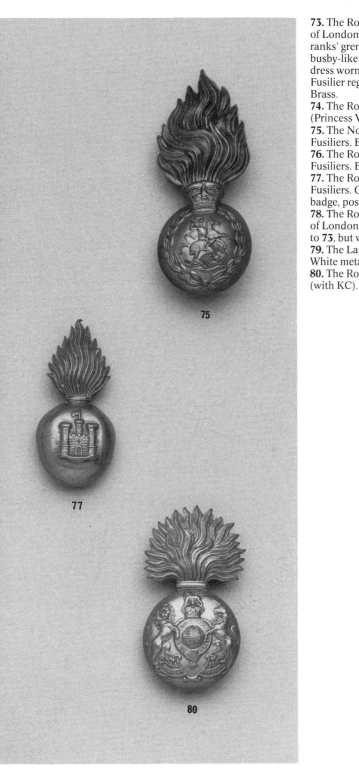

73. The Royal Fusiliers (City of London Regiment). Other ranks' grenade badge for the busby-like racoon skin head-dress worn by the various Fusilier regiments post-1901. Brass.
74. The Royal Irish Fusiliers (Princess Victoria's). Brass.
75. The Northumberland Fusiliers. Brass.
76. The Royal Welsh Fusiliers. Brass.
77. The Royal Inniskilling Fusiliers. Officers' glengarry badge, post-1881. Brass.
78. The Royal Fusiliers (City of London Regiment). Similar to **73**, but with QVC.
79. The Lancashire Fusiliers. White metal.
80. The Royal Scots Fusiliers (with KC).

35

81   82   83   84

86   87   88

90   91   92

95

96

81. The Royal Flying Corps. Unusual other ranks' badge with slider. Brass.
82. RFC. The more usual form, with lugs to secure it to cap.
83. RAF. Cap badge with KC. Brass.
84. RAF. Cap badge introduced in 1942. Plastic, secured by two bendable brass strips.
85. The Army Air Corps, 1957. Anodized.
86. RAF. Cap badge with QC, 1953. Brass.
87. The Army Air Corps, worn 1942–50. Unusual in that it is of hallmarked silver.
88. RAF. Physical Training Instructors' sleeve badge. Brass.
89. The Parachute Regiment. Badge worn from 1943 until 1953 when QC was adopted. White metal.
90. RAF. Officers' badge for peaked cap.
91. RAF. Officers' Dress helmet badge. Bimetal.
92. The Glider Pilot Regiment. Badge with slider adopted in 1955. Anodized.
93. The Parachute Regiment. Collar dogs, pre-1953.
94. The Glider Pilot Regiment. Earlier version.
95. Special Air Service Regiment. Brass badge with wire fittings.
96. SAS. Badge worn from 1953. Bimetal.
97. RAF. Sleeve badge worn by Wireless Operators, Radio and Wireless Mechanics. Cloth.

98

99

100

102

103

104

107

108

109

112

113

114

98. Leeds Rifles (Cockburn High School Cadets). Brass.
99. The 5th (Cinque Ports) Battalion, The Royal Sussex Regiment. White metal.
100. The 6th City of London Battalion (City of London Rifles). Bronze.
101. The 5th City of London Battalion (Rifle Brigade). White metal.
102. The Rifle Brigade (Prince Consort's Own). Badge worn 1934–57. White metal.
103. The King's Royal Rifle Corps. With KC. Black.
104. The Buckinghamshire Battalion, The Oxfordshire and Buckinghamshire Light Infantry. Black.
105. 3/4th County of London Yeomanry (Sharpshooters). Bimetal.
106. The 23rd County of London Battalion, The London Regiment. Bimetal.
107. The 16th County of London Battalion (Queen's Westminster Rifles). Worn 1908–22. Black.
108. The Queen's Royal Rifles. Worn 1961. Brass.
109. The 9th County of London Battalion (Queen Victoria's). Brass.
110. The 3rd County of London (Sharp Shooters) Imperial Yeomanry.
111. The 7th City of London Battalion. Bimetal.
112. The 11th County of London Battalion (Finsbury Rifles). Brass.
113. The 12th County of London Battalion (The Rangers). Black.
114. The King's Royal Rifle Corps Cadets. The motto *Celer et Audax* beneath the crown replaced by *Fight the Good Fight* and *CLB Cadets.*
115. The 21st County of London Battalion (First Surrey Rifles). Black.
116. The 3rd County of London Yeomanry (The Sharpshooters) (Hussars).

117

118

120

121

123

125

126

119

122

124

127

117. The Cameronians
(Scottish Rifles). Piper's
badge, 1921–68. White metal.
118. The Northumberland
Fusiliers: 20th, 21st, 22nd and
29th Battalions (Tyneside
Scottish), 1914–18. White
metal.
119. The Scottish Horse. A
composite badge, possibly for
a slouch hat.
120. The Cameronians
(Scottish Rifles). White metal.
121. The Lowland Brigade.
Worn 1959–68. Anodized.
122. Lovat's Scouts. Worn
1903–20. White metal.
123. The 9th (Glasgow Highlanders) Battalion, The Highland Light Infantry (City of
Glasgow Regiment). Post-
1953. White metal.
124. The 10th (Scottish) Battalion, The King's (Liverpool)
Regiment. Worn 1908–37.
White metal.
125. The Highland Regiment.
Other ranks' badge worn
from 1942 until disbanded in
1949. White metal.
126. The Lowland Regiment.
Similar dates. White metal.
127. The Seaforth High-
landers (Ross-shire Buffs, The
Duke of Albany's). Badge
worn 1898–1921. White
metal.

128

129

133   134   135

137   138

128. The Militia Artillery. Helmet plate worn from 1891 when the title Militia Artillery replaced Artillery Militia. White metal.

129. The Territorial Force. Artillery helmet plate. Laurel spray above gun replaces motto *Ubique* found on plates of the regular units.

130. The Honourable Artillery Company. Officers' forage cap badge, post-1902. Gilded.

131. The Honourable Artillery Company. Worn by Warrant Officers and sergeants. Initials in white metal.

132. The Honourable Artillery Company. Other ranks' cap badge. Brass.

133. The Royal Horse Artillery. Collar dog with KC, 1936–53.

134/5. The Royal Horse Artillery. A pair of collar dogs with QC, 1953.

136. Royal Artillery. Cap badge with KC. Brass.

137. A Cadet Company. Helmet plate with QVC so pre-1901.

138. Cinque Ports Artillery Volunteers. Helmet plate with QVC.

139. Royal Malta Artillery. With KC.

140. Royal Artillery. Badge with KC. Wheel on gun mounted separately.

141

143

145

142

144

146

141. The Royal Marine Light Infantry. Helmet plate worn from 1905. Brass.
142. The Royal East Middlesex Militia. Glengarry badge, 1874–81. White metal.
143. The Royal Malta Militia. Shako plate with KC. Bimetal.
144. The 11th (Royal Militia Island of Jersey) Battalion, The Hampshire Regiment. This unit was only in being from 1940 until 1946.
145. The Middlesex Regiment. Helmet plate with KC (lacking top cross). Bimetal.
146. The Royal Malta Militia. Bimetal.

147   148   149

151   152   153

155   156   157

159   160   161

150

154

158

162   163

147. The Royal Engineers. Forage cap badge with cipher of King George V. The centre was left unvoided as an economy measure during the First World War.
148. Similar badge, with cipher of King George VI and voided centre.
149. Similar badge with cipher of white metal.
150. The Machine Gun Corps. Cap badge, 1915–22.
151. The Royal Army Medical Corps. Cap badge with KC. Brass.
152. RAMC. Badge with St Edward's crown, adopted 1953. Bimetal.
153. The Army Service Corps. Badge worn from 1916 until 1918 when the prefix Royal was added. Brass.
154. The Machine Gun Corps. Officers' collar dog. Bronze.
155. RAMC. Badge with St. Edward's crown, adopted in 1953. Brass.
156. Royal Army Service Corps. Badge with King George VI cipher and voided centre.
157. The Royal Corps of Transport, formed in 1965. Anodized.
158. Crossed axes worn by pioneers in the Infantry, and in some units combined with grenade (Guards), a star (Scots and Irish Guards) and a bugle (light infantry or rifle regiments). Brass.
159. The School of Musketry. Badge worn 1902–19.
160. The Army Physical Training Staff. Forage cap badge worn from 1902.
161. Smaller version of same badge.
162. What appears to be a British collar dog is in fact Belgian. Take care!
163. Artificers' badge worn by armourer sergeants, machinery artificers and smiths.

164   165   166

168   169   170

172   173   174

176   177   178

167

171

175

179

164. The 1/1st London Divisional Cyclist Company, formed in 1916. Voided badge. Brass.

165. The Army Cyclist Corps, formed in 1914. The wheel has 16 spokes; another version has 12. Brass.

166. The 25th County of London (Cyclist) Battalion. Brass.

167. The 15th County of London Battalion (Prince of Wales's Own Civil Service Rifles). Badge worn from 1908. Brass.

168. Inns of Court OTC, incorporating the badges of the various Inns or legal centres of London. Brass.

169. The 5th City of London Battalion (London Rifle Brigade), Cadets. Post-1908. Brass.

170. The Westminster (Yeomanry) Dragoons. Badge worn 1908–22. White metal.

171. The 13th County of London Battalion (Kensington).

172. The Paddington Rifles, 1908–12 when it was replaced by The 10th County of London Regiment (Hackney).

173. The 19th County of London Battalion (St Pancras). Brass.

174. The 20th County of London Battalion (Blackheath and Woolwich). Bimetal.

175. The 18th County of London Battalion (London Irish Rifles). White metal.

176. City of London Imperial Yeomanry (Rough Riders). Bimetal.

177. The 14th County of London Battalion (London Scottish). Worn 1908. White metal.

178. The 10th County of London Battalion (Hackney), post-1912. This unit replaced The Paddington Rifles (see 172). Brass.

179. The 28th County of London Battalion (Artists' Rifles). White metal.

180

181

184

185

186

187

190

191

192

194

195

196

197

198

182

183

188

189

193

199

180. The Life Guards. Centre voided with cipher of King George VI. This unit was formed in 1922 when the 1st and 2nd Life Guards were amalgamated.

181. The 2nd Life Guards, with cipher of King George V, first issued in 1914. Brass.

182. The Scots Guards. Brass.

183. The Scots Guards. Badge worn by sergeants and musicians. White metal.

184. The Life Guards, with cipher of Queen Elizabeth II, post-1953.

185. The 1st Life Guards.

186. The Royal Horse Guards (The Blues), post-1953.

187. The Blues and Royals. Regiment formed in 1969 by amalgamation of The Royal Horse Guards (The Blues) and The Royal Dragoons (1st Dragoons). Brass.

188. Irish Guards. Brass.

189. The Coldstream Guards. Other ranks', 1905–. Brass.

190. The Household Cavalry. Cipher of Queen Elizabeth II.

191. The Grenadier Guards. Flaming grenade; plain for other ranks.

192. The Grenadier Guards. Similar, but with lugs in place of the slider.

193. The Scots Guards. Badge with lugs for attachment to belt or pouch. White metal.

194. The Grenadier Guards. With impressed GR cipher mirrored. Worn by sergeants.

195. The Grenadier Guards. Royal cipher applied and not impressed. Worn by sergeants and commissioned quartermasters. White metal.

196. The Welsh Guards. Shoulder title. White metal.

197. The Welsh Guards. Cap badge worn from 1915 when the regiment was formed. Brass.

198. The Welsh Guards. Badge worn on the puggaree. Brass.

199. The Grenadier Guards. This badge was also worn on the puggaree or, as shown, with the initials GG as a shoulder title. Brass.

200

201

203

206

207

204

208

209

210

211

213

214

216

217

200. The Royal Armoured Corps. Plastic, 1943.
201. The Royal Armoured Corps. White metal, from 1953.
202. Army Remount Service. Bimetal.
203. The 18th (Victoria Mary, Princess of Wales's Own) Hussars. Other ranks', 1905–10. The title was changed in 1911, and the regiment was amalgamated with The 13th Hussars in 1922.
204. The Reconnaissance Corps. White metal, 1942–6.
205. Army Motor Reserve. Brass.
206. The 21st (Empress of India's) Lancers, 1901–22.
207. The 25th Dragoons, 1941–8.
208. The Tank Corps, formed in 1917. Brass.
209. The Royal Tank Corps. White metal badge introduced in 1922 when corps received prefix 'Royal' and motto *Fear Naught*. There are two versions with tanks facing opposite directions.
210. Post-1953 version of badge.
211. The Royal Armoured Corps, 1939–41.
212. The 19th (Queen Alexandra's Own Royal) Hussars. White metal, 1898–1902.
213. The Tank Corps. Sleeve badge. Brass.
214. The Tank Corps. Officers' version. Bronze.
215. The 23rd Hussars. Bi-metal, 1941–8.
216. The Royal Tank Regiment. Shoulder tab. Cloth.
217. The Royal Tank Regiment. Shoulder title. Brass.
218. The 18th (Queen Mary's Own) Royal Hussars. 1910–19.
219. The 19th (Queen Alexandra's Own Royal) Hussars. 1909–22 (see 212).

220

221

222

225

226

227

230

231

232

235

236

237

220. The 3rd (King's Own) Hussars. Bimetal, 1920–58.
221. The 10th Royal Hussars. Bimetal, 1896–1969.
222. The Royal Scots Dragoon Guards. Bimetal, 1971.
223. The 14th (King's) Hussars. Until 1915.
224. The 6th Dragoon Guards (Carabineers). Bimetal, 1902–22.
225. The 8th (King's Royal Irish) Hussars. Bimetal, 1904–54.
226. The 11th (Prince Albert's Own) Hussars. Until 1969.
227. The 7th (The Princess Royal's) Dragoon Guards. 1898–1906.
228. The 15th (The King's) Hussars. Bimetal, 1902–22.
229. The 1st (Royal) Dragoons. 1902–22.
230. The 6th (Inniskilling) Dragoons. Bimetal, until 1922.
231. The 4th (Queen's Own) Hussars. 1907–54.
232. The 7th (Queen's Own) Hussars. 1901–55.
233. The 5th (Princess Charlotte of Wales's) Dragoon Guards. Bimetal, 1902–22.
234. The 13th Hussars. Bimetal, 1902–22.
235. The 5th (Royal Irish) Lancers. Bimetal, 1896–22.
236. The 16th (The Queen's) Lancers. Bimetal, 1905–22.
237. The 9th Queen's Royal Lancers. Anodized, 1954–60.
238. The 12th Royal Lancers (Prince of Wales's). Bimetal, 1930–54.
239. The Royal Dragoons (1st Dragoons). Bimetal, 1949–69.

240

241

242

245

246

247

250

251

252

255

256

257

240. The Royal Berkshire (Hungerford) Yeomanry (Dragoons). Brass, 1908–22.
241. Berkshire Imperial Yeomanry. White metal, 1901–08.
242. The Queen's Own West Kent Yeomanry (Hussars). 1908–22.
243. The 22nd Dragoons. White metal, 1940–8.
244. The 26th Hussars. Brass, 1940–8.
245. The Scottish Horse. Raised in 1900 for the Imperial Yeomanry. Brass.
246. Similar badge with Scottish crown. White metal.
247. The Queen Mary's Surrey Yeomanry (Lancers). 1910–22. White metal.
248. The 21st (Empress of India's) Lancers. Economy brass issue from 1916.
249. The 24th Lancers. White metal, 1940–8.
250. The Fife and Forfarshire Yeomanry (Dragoons). Found in brass and white metal, 1908–22.
251. The Hertfordshire Yeomanry (Dragoons). Brass, 1908–22.
252. The Bedfordshire and Hertfordshire Regiment. Bimetal, 1919–58.
253. The 20th Hussars. 1908–22. Brass.
254. The 27th Lancers. Bimetal, 1940–8.
255. The Queen Mary's Surrey Yeomanry (Lancers). With voided centre (see 247).
256. The Royal Gloucestershire Hussars (a unit of the Imperial Yeomanry). 1902–8.
257. The Duke of Connaught's Own Royal East Kent Yeomanry (Mounted Rifles). 1908–22.
258. The 17th (Duke of Cambridge's Own) Lancers. NCOs' arm badge. White metal.
259. Similar badge in brass. In 1922 the regiment was amalgamated with The 21st (Empress of India's) Lancers to form The 17th/21st Lancers.

260

261

262

264

265

266

267

269

270

271

273

274

275

276

263

268

272

277

260. The Royal Irish Rifles. White metal, 1913–52. The title was changed to The Royal Ulster Rifles in 1920.
261. The Royal Irish Rangers. Anodized, 1968.
262. The North Irish Horse. Brass, 1908–52.
263. The Dublin County Light Infantry. Glengarry badge, post-1881. White metal.
264. The Connaught Rangers. Officers' badge, 1902–22. Bronze.
265. The 8th Irish Battalion, The King's (Liverpool Regiment). Brass, 1908–21.
266. The Connaught Rangers. Brass, 1902–22.
267. The Northumberland Fusiliers: 24th–27th and 30th Battalions (Tyneside Irish), 1914–18. Brass.
268. The Dublin Regiment National Volunteers. Brass.
269. The Royal Dublin Fusiliers. Officers' badge, 1881–1922. Bronze.
270. The North of Ireland Imperial Yeomanry. Collar dog, 1901–8. White metal.
271. The Royal Dublin Fusiliers. Bimetal, 1881–1922.
272. The 14th Battalion (Young Citizens), The Royal Irish Rifles. Brass, 1914–18.
273. The Royal Ulster Rifles. White metal, 1920. Doubtful if original badge.
274. The Royal Munster Fusiliers. Bimetal, 1898–1921.
275. The Prince of Wales's Leinster Regiment (Royal Canadians). Bimetal, 1881–1922.
276. The Royal Inniskilling Fusiliers. Bimetal, 1881–1958; except during the late 1920s and early 1930s when the grenade was discarded.
277. The South Irish Horse. Brass, 1908–22.

278

279

282

283

285

286

288

289

280

281

284

287

290

278. The King's Own Scottish Borderers. White metal, 1887–1902.
279. The King's Own Scottish Borderers. White metal, post–1902.
280. The Highland Light Infantry. With small scroll, white metal, 1902–52.
281. The Highland Light Infantry. With large scroll, white metal, 1902–52.
282. The Queen's Own Cameron Highlanders. White metal, 1898–1961.
283. The Queen's Own Cameron Highlanders. Badge for feather bonnet and glengarry. White metal.
284. The Queen's Own Cameron Highlanders (The Liverpool Scottish). White metal, post-1938.
285. The Argyll and Sutherland Highlanders (Princess Louise's). Officers' collar dog. Bronze.
286. The Argyll and Sutherland Highlanders (Princess Louise's). Other ranks' collar dog. White metal.
287. The Royal Scots (Royal Regiment). Bimetal with red (1st Battalion) or green (2nd Battalion) cloth backing at centre, 1920–58, and from 1969.
288. The Princess Louise's (Argyll and Sutherland Highlanders). White metal with solid centre, 1882–1900.
289. Similar, but with voided centre.
290. The Highland Brigade. Anodized, 1959–68.

291

292

293

296

297

298

300

301

304

305

306

291. Oxford University OTC (Infantry). White metal.
292. The King's (Shropshire Light Infantry). Bimetal.
293. The Duke of Cornwall's Light Infantry. White metal.
294. The Women's Army Auxiliary Corps, formed in 1917. Brass.
295. Auxiliary Territorial Service (women's service formed in 1938). Brass.
296. Prince Albert's (Somerset Light Infantry). White metal.
297. Prince Albert's (Somerset Light Infantry): 4th and 5th Battalions.
298. The Durham Light Infantry. White metal, 1902–53.
299. The Royal Observer Corps.
300. The York and Lancaster Regiment. Bimetal, 1881–1969.
301. The Cambridgeshire Regiment. Formed in 1908. Bimetal. The title is also found spelt as Cambridgshire.
302. The Women's Legion. Formed in 1915 and absorbed into the WAAC in 1917. White metal.
303. The Women's Land Army. Reformed in 1939. With green enamel centre.
304. The King's Own Yorkshire Light Infantry. Bimetal, 1898–1958.
305. The Loyal North Lancashire Regiment. Bimetal, 1901–20.
306. The Loyal (North Lancashire) Regiment. Bimetal, 1921–53.
307. Queen Alexandra's Royal Army Nursing Corps. 1949–53.
308. Queen Mary's Army Auxiliary Corps and Army Territorial Service, Old Comrades' Association.

309

310

311

313

314

315

317

318

319

321

322

323

312

316

320

324

309. The Sherwood Foresters (The Derbyshire Regiment). Bimetal, 1898–1901.
310. The Sherwood Foresters (The Derbyshire Regiment). Belt or pouch fitting. Bimetal.
311. The 4th Battalion, Duke of Edinburgh's (The Wiltshire Regiment). Black, 1916–47.
312. The Border Regiment. White metal, 1901–53.
313. The Sherwood Foresters (Nottinghamshire and Derbyshire Regiment). Officers' badge, 1902–53. Bronze.
314. The Essex Volunteer Regiment. Brass, 1914–18.
315. The East Anglian Brigade. Formed in 1957/8 and changed to The Royal Anglian Regiment in 1968. White metal.
316. The 5th Battalion, The Border Regiment. White metal, with South Africa battle honour.
317. The Northamptonshire Regiment. With castle and flag. Brass, 1898–1921.
318. The Northamptonshire Regiment. Without flag and key. Bimetal.
319. The Essex Regiment. Bronze, 1908–58.
320. The Prince of Wales's Volunteers (The South Lancashire Regiment). Bimetal, 1920–58.
321. The Duke of Cambridge's Own (Middlesex Regiment). Bimetal, 1898–1921.
322. The same badge, but plastic, *circa* 1943.
323. The East Yorkshire Regiment. Bimetal, 1898–1958.
324. The 2nd King Edward's Horse. Brass, 1914–24.

325

326

327

330

331

332

335

336

337

339

340

341

325. The Duke of Lancaster's Own Yeomanry (Dragoons). Brass, 1908–51.
326. The South Nottinghamshire (Yeomanry) Hussars. Brass, 1908–52.
327. Westmoreland and Cumberland Yeomanry. Brass, 1908–22.
328. The Lincolnshire Yeomanry (Lancers). Brass, 1908–22.
329. The Prince Albert's Own Leicestershire Yeomanry (Hussars). Brass, 1922–56.
330. The Essex Yeomanry. Brass, 1916–54.
331. The Imperial Yeomanry. General Service badge worn on the slouch hat, 1901–8. Brass, with red and blue rosette.
332. The Duke of Lancaster's Own Yeomanry (Dragoons). Bimetal.
333. The Shropshire Yeomanry. Brass, 1908–50.
334. The Earl of Chester's Cheshire Yeomanry (Hussars). Brass, 1908–22.
335. The Queen's Own (Royal West Kent) Regiment. White metal, 1898–1958.
336. The Queen's Own Yorkshire Yeomanry (Dragoons). White metal, 1951–6.
337. The 1st Battalion, The Monmouthshire Regiment. White metal, 1908–25.
338. The Queen's Own Worcestershire (Yeomanry) Hussars. Bimetal, 1908–56.
339. The Brecknockshire Battalion, The South Wales Borderers. Brass, 1908–22.
340. The Duke of York's Own Loyal Suffolk (Yeomanry) Hussars. Bimetal, 1908–61.
341. The Glamorganshire Yeomanry (Dragoons). Bimetal, 1908–22.
342. The Derbyshire Yeomanry (Dragoons). Brass, 1908–57.

343

344

345

348

349

350

353

354

355

358

359

360

343. The Dorsetshire Regiment. Bimetal, 1898–1901.
344. The Dorsetshire Regiment. Bimetal, 1901–56.
345. The Royal Warwickshire Regiment. Bimetal, 1898–1958.
346. The Hampshire Yeomanry (Carabineers). Brass, 1916–51.
347. The Northumberland (Yeomanry) Hussars. Brass, 1908–56.
348. The Duke of Wellington's (West Riding Regiment). Officers' collar dog. Bronze.
349. The Prince of Wales's Own (West Yorkshire Regiment). Bimetal, 1898–1958.
350. The Duke of Wellington's (West Riding Regiment). Bimetal, 1897–1970.
351. The Alexandra, Princess of Wales's Own Yorkshire Yeomanry (Hussars). Bimetal, 1908–56.
352. The 2nd Northamptonshire Yeomanry. White metal, 1939–45.
353. Alexandra, Princess of Wales's Own (Yorkshire Regiment). Brass, 1898–1908.
354. The East Lancashire Regiment. Officers' collar dog. Bronze.
355. The East Lancashire Regiment. Bimetal, 1930–54.
356. The Welsh (Yeomanry) Horse (Lancers). Brass, 1914–21.
357. The Pembrokeshire (Castlemain) Yeomanry (Hussars). Bimetal, 1908–71.
358. The Green Howards (Alexandra, Princess of Wales's Own Yorkshire Regiment). Bronze, 1903–50.
359. The King's Regiment (Liverpool). Bimetal, 1927–50.
360. The Green Howards (Alexandra, Princess of Wales's Own Yorkshire Regiment). Badge worn 1950–8, and 1969–. Anodized.
361. The Royal Buckinghamshire (Yeomanry) Hussars. Brass, 1908–52.
362. The Huntingdonshire Cyclist Battalion. Brass, 1914–18. Also The Huntingdonshire Home Guard, 1951–7.

363

364

365

368

369

370

372

373

377

376

381

380

382

363. The 7th Battalion, The Hampshire Regiment. Brass, 1908–21.
364. The Cheshire Regiment. Bronze, 1898–1921.
365. The Hampshire Regiment. Officers' pattern. Bimetal.
366. The Lancashire Fusiliers. Officers' badge, 1898–1921. Bronze.
367. The Lancashire Fusiliers. Bimetal, 1898–1921.
368. The Hampshire Regiment. Bimetal, 1898–1921.
369. The Royal Hampshire Regiment. Bimetal, 1947–53.
370. The South Wales Borderers. Bimetal, 1898–1969.
371. The Cheshire Regiment. Bimetal, 1898–1921.
372. The Gloucestershire Regiment. Brass badge worn on rear of head-dress.
373. The Gloucestershire Regiment. White metal, 1898–1958.
374. The Lincolnshire Regiment. Bimetal, 1898–1947.
375. The Bedfordshire Regiment. Brass, 1898–1919.
376. The 4th Battalion, The Gloucestershire Regiment. Blackened brass, 1898–1958.
377. The 8th (Isle of Wight Rifles, Princess Beatrice's) Battalion, The Hampshire Regiment. Black, 1908–21.
378. The Suffolk Regiment. Bimetal, 1901–55.
379. The Welsh Regiment. Bimetal, 1898 until 1920 when it became Welch.
380. The Cheshire Regiment. Bimetal, 1898–1921. See **370** with larger scroll.
381. The Cheshire Regiment. Bimetal, 1922–58 and post-1969.
382. The Prince of Wales's (North Staffordshire Regiment). Bronze, 1898–1959.
383. The Leicestershire Regiment. Bimetal, 1898–1951.

71

384

385

386

388

389

390

392

393

394

395

397

398

384. The Army Educational Corps. Brass, 1927–46.
385. Yeomanry Cadets. KC. Brass.
386. Army Apprentices' School. Piper's badge. White metal, 1954.
387. The Royal Naval Mine Watching Service.
388. The Royal Military Academy, Woolwich. Gilded, gilt and bronze, 1902–47.
389. The Royal Military College, Sandhurst. White metal, 1947–53.
390. The Royal Army Pay Corps. Bimetal, 1929–53.
391. Drake Battalion, The Royal Naval Division. Bimetal, 1916–18.
392. The Royal Army Educational Corps. Bimetal, 1946–54.
393. The Royal Army Educational Corps. Bimetal, 1954–.
394. The Mobile Defence Corps. Bimetal, 1955–9.
395. The Royal Army Pay Corps. Brass, 1920–29.
396. Anson Battalion, The Royal Naval Division. Brass, 1916–18.
397. The Army Catering Corps. Bimetal, 1941–54.
398. The Army Catering Corps. Brass, 1941–54.
399. Royal Navy. Officers' cap badge.

400

401

402

404

405

406

409

410

411

414

415

416

403

408

407

413

412

417

400. The Manchester Regiment. Bimetal, 1898–1923.
401. The Manchester Regiment. Brass, 1923–58. Also in white metal.
402. The Manchester Regiment. Bimetal, 1898–1923. With different style of lettering.
403. The East Anglian Brigade. Anodized, 1958.
404. The Royal Norfolk Regiment. Brass, 1937–58.
405. The Norfolk Regiment. Bimetal, 1898–1937.
406. The Norfolk Regiment. Bronze.
407. The Devonshire Regiment. Bimetal, 1903–55.
408. The Devonshire Regiment. Blackened brass, 1920–47.
409. The Herefordshire Regiment. Bimetal, 1908–47.
410. The Buffs (East Kent Regiment). Brass, 1896–1961.
411. The Herefordshire Regiment. Officers' badge. Bronze.
412. The Royal Northumberland Fusiliers. Bimetal, 1935–59.
413. The Worcestershire Regiment. Bimetal, 1925–66.
414. The Suffolk Regiment. Brass, 1901–52.
415. The Worcestershire Regiment. Brass, 1898–1925.
416. The Suffolk Regiment. White metal.
417. The Northumberland Fusiliers. Brass, pre-1935.

418

419

420

423

424

425

428

429

430

432

433

434

418. The Royal Corps of Signals. Bimetal, 1920–47.
419. The Royal Corps of Signals. Officers' badge. Bronze.
420. Army Ordnance Corps. Brass, 1896–1918.
421. The Intelligence Corps. Brass, 1940–55.
422. The Intelligence Corps. Anodized, 1955.
423. The Royal Army Ordnance Corps. Brass, 1918–47.
424. The Royal Army Ordnance Corps. 1947–49.
425. Oxford University OTC (Signals).
426. Army Veterinary Corps. Brass, 1916.
427. Army Veterinary Corps. Bimetal, 1903–18.
428. The Corps of Royal Military Police. Brass, 1948–53.
429. The Corps of Royal Military Police. Bimetal, 1953.
430. The Military Provost Staff Corps. Brass, 1936–53.
431. Navy, Army and Air Force Institutes (NAAFI). Silver plated.
432. Royal Army Chaplains' Department. Collar dog, 1939–53. Bronze.
433. Army Scripture Readers. Bimetal.
434. Royal Army Dental Corps. Bimetal, 1948–54.
435. Royal Army Dental Corps. Brass, 1921–48.
436. Royal Army Dental Corps. Officers' badge. Bronze.

INDEX TO THE PLATES

Some unit titles have been slightly modified in order to simplify the listing and location of entries, but the relevant captions give the full titles.

Airborne Forces, 53
Air Corps (Army), 85, 87
Air Training Corps, 50
Alexandra, Princess of Wales's Own Yorkshire Regiment, 353, 358, 360
Alexandra, Princess of Wales's Own Yorkshire Yeomanry, 351
Anson Battalion, Royal Naval Division, 396
Apprentices' School (Army), 386
Argyll & Sutherland Highlanders (Princess Louise's), 285, 286, 288, 289
Army:
  Air Corps, 85, 87
  Apprentices' School, 386
  Catering Corps, 397, 398
  Educational Corps, 384
  Motor Reserve, 205
  Ordnance Corps, 420
  Physical Training Staff, 160, 161
  Remount Service, 202
  Scripture Readers, 433
  Service Corps, 153, 155
  Veterinary Corps, 426, 427
Artificers, 163
Artillery:
  Honourable Company, 130, 131, 132
  Militia, 128
  Royal, 136, 140
  Royal Cadets, 137
  Horse, 133, 134, 135
  Malta, 139
  Territorial, 129
Artists Rifles, 28th County of

London, 52, 56, 179
Auxiliary Territorial Service, 295

Bedfordshire & Hertfordshire Regiment, 252
Bedfordshire Regiment, 375
Berkshire, 66th Regiment of Foot, 35
Blackheath & Woolwich, 20th County of London, 174
Bloomsbury Rifles, 15, 28
Blues, The Royal Horse Guards, 186
Blues and Royals, 187
Border Regiment, 312, 316
Brecknockshire Battalion, South Wales Borderers, 339
Buckinghamshire Battalion, Oxs. & Bucks Light Infantry, 104
Buffs, Royal East Kent Regiment, 410
Buttons, 39, 40, 41, 42, 44, 45, 46, 47, 48, 49, 50

Cambridgeshire Regiment, 301
Cameronians (Scottish Rifles), 117, 120
Carabineers, 224, 346
Catering Corps, Army, 397, 398
Chaplains' Department, Royal Army, 432
Chelmsford Loyal Volunteers, 7
Cheshire Regiment, 364, 371, 380, 381
Cheshire Yeomanry, 340
Cinque Ports, Artillery Volunteers, 138
Cinque Ports, 5th Battalion, Royal Sussex Regiment, 99
Cinque Ports, Rifle Volunteers, 47

City of London Regiment:
  5th Battalion, 101
  6th Battalion, 100
  7th Battalion, 20, 29, 111
  11th Battalion, 112
Civil Service Rifles, 167
Cockburn High School Cadets, 98
Coldstream Guards, 189
Collar Dogs, 21, 22, 23, 25, 26, 27, 28, 29, 30, 32, 33, 69, 71, 93, 133, 134, 135, 154, 162, 270
Connaught Rangers, 264, 266
Corps of Royal Military Police, 428, 429
County of London Regiment:
  3/4th Battalion, 105
  9th Battalion, 109
  10th Battalion, 178
  11th Battalion, 112
  12th Battalion, 113
  13th Battalion, 171
  14th Battalion, 177
  15th Battalion, 167
  16th Battalion, 107
  18th Battalion, 175
  19th Battalion, 173
  20th Battalion, 174
  21st Battalion, 115
  22nd Battalion, 64
  23rd Battalion, 106
  24th Battalion, 18
  25th Battalion, 166
  28th Battalion, 179
Cranleigh School CCF, 65
Cyclists:
  1st London, 164
  25th County of London, 166
  Army Corps, 165
  Huntingdonshire Battalion, 362

Dental Corps, Royal Army, 434, 435, 436
Derbyshire Regiment, 309, 310
Derbyshire Yeomanry (Dragoons), 342
Devizes Association, 3
Devon, North, 11th Regiment of Foot, 2
Devonshire Regiment, 407, 408
Dorsetshire Regiment, 343, 344
Down, Royal County, 86th Regiment of Foot, 14
Dragoon Guards:
  5th, 233

6th, 224
7th, 227
Dragoons:
  1st, 229, 239
  22nd, 243
  25th, 207
Derbyshire Yeomanry, 342
Duke of Lancaster's Own Yeomanry, 325, 332
Fife & Forfarshire Yeomanry, 250
Glamorganshire Yeomanry, 341
Hertfordshire Yeomanry, 251
Queen's Own Yorkshire Yeomanry, 336
Drake Battalion, Royal Naval Division, 391
Dublin County Light Infantry, 263
Dublin Regiment, National Volunteers, 268
Duke of Cambridge's Own 17th Lancers, 258, 259
Duke of Cambridge's Own Middlesex Regiment, 321, 322
Duke of Connaught's Own Royal East Kent Yeomanry, 257
Duke of Cornwall's Light Infantry, 39, 293
Duke of Edinburgh's Wiltshire Regiment, 311
Duke of Lancaster's Own Yeomanry (Dragoons), 325, 332
Duke of Wellington's West Riding Regiment, 348, 350
Durham Light Infantry, 298

Earl of Chester's Cheshire Yeomanry, 334
East Anglian Brigade, 315, 403
East Kent Regiment, The Buffs, 410
East Lancashire Regiment, 354, 355
East India Volunteers, 6
East Surrey Regiment, 67, 72
East Yorkshire Regiment, 323
Educational Corps, Army, 384
Empress of India's 21st Lancers, 206, 248
Essex Regiment, 319
Essex Volunteer Regiment, 314
Essex Yeomanry, 330

Fife & Forfarshire Yeomanry (Dragoons), 250

Finsbury Rifles, 112
Foot Guards *see* Guards
Fusiliers:
  Lancashire, 79, 366, 367
  Northumberland, 75, 118, 267, 417
  Royal, City of London, 73, 78
  Royal Dublin, 269, 271
  Royal Inniskilling, 77, 276
  Royal Irish, 74
  Royal Munster, 274
  Royal Northumberland, 412
  Royal Scots, 80

General Officers, 44
Glider Pilots Regiment, 92, 94
Glamorganshire Yeomanry
  (Dragoons), 341
Gloucestershire Regiment, 372, 373,
  376
Gordon Highlanders, 27
Green Howards, 358, 360
Grenadier Guards, 191, 192, 194, 195,
  199
Guards:
  Coldstream, 189
  Grenadier, 191, 192, 194, 195, 199
  Irish, 188
  Scots, 182, 183, 193
  Welsh, 196, 197, 198

Hackney Rifles, 10th County of
  London, 178
Hampshire Regiment, 363, 365, 368,
  377
Hampshire Regiment, Jersey
  Battalion, 144
Hampshire Yeomanry, Carabineers,
  346
Herefordshire Regiment, 409, 411
Hertfordshire & Bedfordshire
  Yeomanry, 33
Hertfordshire Yeomanry (Dragoons),
  251
Highland Brigade, 290
Highland Light Infantry, 123, 280,
  281
Highland Regiment, 125
Holborn Battalion, Rifle Volunteers,
  51
Home Guard, 362
Honourable Artillery Company, 130,
  131, 132

Household Cavalry, 190
Hungerford, Royal Berkshire
  Yeomanry, 240
Huntingdonshire Cyclist Battalion,
  362
Hussars:
  3rd, 220
  4th, 231
  7th, 232
  8th, 225
  10th, 221
  11th, 226
  13th, 234
  14th, 223
  15th, 228
  18th, 203, 218
  19th, 212, 219
  20th, 253
  23rd, 215
  26th, 244
  Duke of York's Own Loyal Suffolk
    Yeomanry, 340
  Earl of Chester's Cheshire
    Yeomanry, 334
  King's, 223, 228
  King's Own, 3rd, 220
  Pembrokeshire Yeomanry, 357
  Prince Albert's Own Leicestershire
    Yeomanry, 329
  Princess of Wales's Own Yorkshire
    Yeomanry, 351
  Queen's Own West Kent
    Yeomanry, 242
  Queen's Own Worcestershire
    Yeomanry, 338
  Royal Buckinghamshire Yeomanry,
    361
  Royal Gloucestershire Yeomanry,
    256
  South Notthinghamshire
    Yeomanry, 326

Inniskilling Dragoons, 6th, 230
Inniskilling Fusiliers, Royal, 77, 276
Inns of Court OTC, 168
Intelligence Corps, 421, 422
Irish Guards, 188
Island of Jersey, Royal Militia, 144
Isle of Wight Rifles, 377

Jersey, Island of, Militia, 144

Kensington, 13th County of London, 171

King Edward's Horse, 2nd, 324

King's Hussars, 14th, 223

King's Hussars, 15th, The, 228

King's (Liverpool) Regiment, 124, 265, 359

King's Own Borderers, 25th Regiment of Foot, 12

King's Own Hussars, 3rd, 220

King's Own Royal Lancaster Regiment, 25

King's Own Scottish Borderers, 278, 279

King's Shropshire Light Infantry, 292

King's Own Yorkshire Light Infantry, 304

King's Rifle Corps, 103

King's Rifle Corps Cadets, 114

King's Royal Irish, 8th Hussars, 225

Lancashire Fusiliers, 79, 366, 367

Lancaster Regiment, King's Own Royal, 25

Lancers:
5th, 235
9th, 237
12th, 238
16th, 236
17th, 258
21st, 206, 248
24th, 249
27th, 254
Lincolnshire Yeomanry, 328
Queen Mary's Surrey Yeomanry, 247, 255
Welsh (Yeomanry) Horse, 356

Leeds Rifles, Cockburn High School Cadets, 98

Leicestershire 17th Regiment of Foot, 1

Leicestershire Regiment, 383

Leicestershire Yeomanry, 329

Leinster Regiment, 275

Life Guards, 180, 184

Life Guards, 1st, 185

Life Guards, 2nd, 181

Lincolnshire Regiment, 23, 374

Lincolnshire Yeomanry (Lancers), 328

Liverpool Scottish, 284

London & Westminster Light Horse, 5, 43

London Irish Rifles, 18th County of London, 175

London Regiment: see City of London Regiment and County of London Regiment

London Rifle Brigade Cadets, 169

London Scottish, 177

Lovat's Scouts, 122

Lowland Brigade, 121

Lowland Regiment, 126

Loyal North Lancashire Regiment, 305, 306

Machine Gun Corps, 150, 154

Manchester Regiment, 400, 401, 402

Medical Staff, 46

Metropolitan Special Constabulary, 55

Middlesex Regiment, 145, 321, 322

Military Police, Corps of, 428, 429

Military Provost Staff Corps, 430

Militia, 128, 142, 143, 144, 146

Mobile Defence Corps, 394

Monmouthshire Regiment, 337

Motor Reserve, Army, 205

NAAFI, 43

Norfolk, 9th Regiment of Foot, 11

Norfolk Regiment, 16, 17, 30, 36, 37, 405, 406

Northamptonshire Regiment, 22, 317, 318

Northamptonshire Yeomanry, 352

North Irish Horse, 262

North Lincoln, 10th Regiment of Foot, 31

North of Ireland Imperial Yeomanry, 270

Northumberland Fusiliers, 75, 118, 267, 417

Northumberland Yeomanry, Hussars, 347

North Staffordshire Regiment, 382

Nottinghamshire & Derbyshire Regiment, 313

Ordnance Corps, Army, 420

Ordnance Store, 42

Oxford University OTC, 32, 291, 425

Oxford University Rifle Volunteers, 45

Paddington Rifles, 172
Parachute Regiment, 89, 93
Pembrokeshire Yeomanry, 357
Physical Training Instructors (RAF), 88
Physical Training Staff (Army), 160, 161
Pioneers, 158
Police, Corps of Military, 428, 429
Provost Staff Corps, Military, 430
Prince Albert's Own 11th Hussars, 226
Prince Albert's Own Leicestershire Yeomanry Hussars, 329
Prince Albert's Own Somersetshire Light Infantry, 296, 297
Prince Consort's Own, 102
Prince of Wales's 12th Lancers, 238
Prince of Wales's Leinster Regiment, 275
Prince of Wales's North Staffordshire Regiment, 382
Prince of Wales's Own Civil Service Rifles, 167
Prince of Wales's South Lancashire Volunteers, 320
Prince of Wales's West Yorkshire Regiment, 349
Princess Beatrice's Isle of Wight Rifles, 377
Princess Charlotte of Wales's Dragoon Guards, 233
Princess Louise's Argyll & Sutherland Highlanders, 285, 286, 288, 289
Princess of Wales's Own 18th Hussars, 203
Princess of Wales's Own Yorkshire Yeomanry, 351
Princess Royal's 7th Dragoon Guards, 227
Princess Victoria's Royal Irish Fusiliers, 74

Queen Alexandra's Own Royal Hussars, 212, 219
Queen Alexandra's Royal Army Nursing Corps, 307
Queen Mary's Army Auxiliary Corps & Army Territorial Service, 308

Queen Mary's Own Royal Hussars, 18th, 218
Queen Mary's Surrey Yeomanry (Lancers), 247, 255
Queen Victoria's 9th County of London Battalion, 109
Queen's 22nd County of London Battalion, 64
Queen's Lancers, 16th, 236
Queen's Own Hussars, 4th, 231
Queen's Own Hussars, 7th, 232
Queen's Own Royal West Kent, 335
Queen's Own West Kent Yeomanry, 242
Queen's Own Worcestershire Yeomanry, 338
Queen's Own Yorkshire Yeomanry (Dragoons), 336
Queen's Regiment, 68
Queen's Royal Lancers, 9th, 237
Queen's Royal Regiment, 2nd of Foot, 8, 57, 58, 59, 60, 61, 62, 63, 64, 66, 69, 71
Queen's Royal Rifles, 108
Queen's Royal Surrey Regiment, 70
Queen's Westminster Rifles, 107

Rangers, 113
Readers, Army Scripture, 433
Reconnaissance Corps, 204
Regiments of Foot:
  2nd, 8, 57
  9th, 11, 13
  10th, 31
  11th, 2
  17th, 1
  25th, 12
  62nd, 9
  66th, 35
  80th, 34
  86th, 14
Remount Service, 202
Rifle Brigade, 102
Rifle Volunteers, 45, 47, 51
Rough Riders, 176
Royal Air Force, 26, 48, 49, 83, 84, 86, 88, 90, 91, 97
Royal Army:
  Chaplains' Department, 432
  Dental Corps, 434, 435, 436
  Educational Corps, 392, 393
  Medical Corps, 151, 152, 155

Ordnance Corps, 423, 424
Pay Corps, 390, 395
Service Corps, 156
Royal:
Anglian Regiment, 315
Armoured Corps, 200, 201, 211
Artillery, 136, 140
Berkshire Yeomanry, 240
Buckinghamshire Yeomanry
(Hussars), 361
Corps of Signals, 418, 419
Corps of Transport, 157
Dublin Fusiliers, 269, 271
East Middlesex Militia, 142
Engineers, 147, 148, 149
Engineers' Department, 40
Flying Corps, 81, 82
Fusiliers, 38
Fusiliers, City of London, 73, 78
Gloucestershire Yeomanry
(Hussars), 256
Hampshire Regiment, 369
Horse Artillery, 133, 134, 135
Horse Guards, The Blues, 186
Hussars, 10th, 221
Inniskilling Fusiliers, 77, 276
Irish Fusiliers, 74
Irish Lancers, 5th, 235
Irish Rangers, 261
Irish Rifles, 260, 272
Malta Militia, 143, 146
Marine Light Infantry, 141
Military Academy, Woolwich, 388
Military College, Sandhurst, 389
Military Police, Corps of, 428, 429
Militia, Island of Jersey, 144
Naval Mine Watching Service, 387
Munster Fusiliers, 274
Naval Division, 391, 396
Norfolk Regiment, 404
Northumberland Fusiliers, 118,
267, 412
Observer Corps, 299
Scots, 287
Scots Dragoon Guards, 222
Scots Fusiliers, 80
Sussex Regiment, 99
Tank Regiment, 216, 217
Ulster Rifles, 260, 273
Warwickshire Regiment, 345
Welsh Fusiliers, 76
West Surrey Regiment, 19

Royal Navy, 399

Saint Pancras, 19th County of
London Battalion, 173
School of Musketry, 159
Scots Guards, 182, 183, 193
Scottish Horse, 119, 245, 246
Scripture Readers, Army, 433
Seaforth Highlanders, 127
Service Corps, Army, 153
Sharpshooters, 105, 110, 116
Sherwood Foresters, 309, 310, 313
Shropshire Light Infantry, 292
Signals, Royal Corps of, 418, 419
Somerset Light Infantry, 296, 297
South Irish Horse, 277
South Lancashire Volunteers, 320
South Nottinghamshire Yeomanry
(Hussars), 326
South Wales Borderers, 339, 370
Special Air Service Regiment, 95, 96
Special services (1914–18), 54
Staffordshire Volunteers, 34
Suffolk Regiment, 378, 414, 416
Suffolk Yeomanry, 340
Surrey Rifles, 21st County of London
Battalion, 115

Tank Corps, 21, 208, 209, 210, 213,
214
The King's Hussars, 15th, 228
Tyneside Irish, 267
Tyneside Scottish, 118

Veterinary Corps (Army), 426, 427

Waist belt fittings, 19, 31, 35, 36, 37,
38, 52
Welsh, 41st Regiment of Foot, 10
Welsh Guards, 196, 197, 198
Welsh Horse Yeomanry (Lancers),
356
Welsh Regiment, 379
Westminster Yeomanry, 170
Westmoreland & Cumberland
Yeomanry, 327
West Riding, Duke of Wellington's
Regiment, 348, 350
West Surrey Regiment, 19, 24
West Yorkshire Regiment, 349
Wiltshire, 62nd Regiment of Foot, 9
Wiltshire Regiment, 311

Women's Auxiliary Army Corps, 294
Women's Land Army, 303
Women's Legion, 302
Worcestershire Regiment, 413, 415

Yeomanry:
  Berkshire Imperial, 241
  Cadets, 385
  Cheshire, 340
  City of London Imperial, 176
  County of London, 105
  Derbyshire, 342
  Duke of Lancaster's Own, 325, 332
  Duke of York's Own, 340
  Earl of Chester's, 334
  Essex, 330
  Fife & Forfarshire, 250
  Glamorganshire, 341
  Hampshire, 346
  Hertfordshire, 251
  Hertfordshire & Bedfordshire, 33
  Imperial, 331
  Lincolnshire, 328
  Leicestershire, 329
  Northamptonshire, 352
  Northumberland, 347
  Queen's Own Worcestershire, 338
  Royal Berkshire, 240
  Royal Buckinghamshire, 361
  Sharpshooters, 110, 116
  Shropshire, 333
  South Nottinghamshire, 326
  Welsh, 356
  Westminster, 170
  Westmoreland & Cumberland, 327
  Yorkshire, 336, 351
York & Lancaster Regiment, 300